PALM LEAVES

An Anthology of Three Emerging Ghanaian Poets

Contributing Poets

Nana Arhin Tsiwah
Nene Tetteh Adusu
Kofi Acquah

First Published in 2016
Published by:
FORTE Publications
#12 Ashmun Street
Snapper Hill
Monrovia, Liberia

FORTE Publishing
7202 Tavenner Lane
208 Alexandria
VA, 22306

FORTE Press
76 Sarasit Road
Ban Pong, 70110
Ratchaburi, Thailand

An Agyemang Duah Publication

http://fortepublishing.wix.com/fppp

This book or any portion thereof may not be reproduced or used in any manner whatsoever without the express written permission of the publisher except for the use of brief quotations in a book review.

Printed in the United States of America

Copyright © 2016 FORTE Publications
All rights reserved.

ISBN: 0994534736
ISBN-13: 978-0-9945347-3-6

Dedication

Dedicated to all the poets of Ghana
that keep the tradition alive. .

Contents

Table of Contents
Dedication... iii
Contents... v
Notes.. ix
*15 poems by **Nana Arhin Tsiwah** x
These Are Mothers: Some Dead, Some Alive...... 1
This Home: A Warmed Song....................... 5
When We Have Reached Home..................... 6
Three Hundred Fables 8
A Traveler's Recital............................... 9
Confrontational................................... 10
Salaga 11
Badu.. 13
Afarfo 14
Ekuafo.. 15
Antobam.. 16
Abrebrese 17
Plea Without Help 19
*15 Poems by **Nene Tetteh Adusu** 20
A Great Tree...................................... 21
Frogged.. 22
Candle... 23
Today: Tomorrow.................................. 24
Nightmare... 25
Africa: *Slowly* And *Quietly* 26
One More Hymn (For Kofi Awoonor).............. 28
Peace, Where It Lies?............................ 30
A Sin, Poverty..................................... 31
Ire 32
Disquiet 33
Stolen Moments................................... 34
Broken... 35
Joy Lost Found.................................... 36
Gazing, Glancing, and Guessing.................. 38

*15 poems by **Kofi Acquah** 39
In The Silent River 40
Yaanom 42
A Broken Pot 43
Shadows From The West 45
Stuck to the fetish 46
Fie Nyimpa 47
Under The Village Hut 49
Koryɛ 51
Pull The Trigger 53
The Village Boys 54
Here We Sit 56
Jumping The Pit 58
Cultured Old Days 59
Preservers 60
Laughing Cowries 61
   ABOUT CONTRIBUTING POETS 62

NANA ARHIN TSIWAH 63
NENE TETTEH ADUSU 64
KOFI ACQUAH 65

PALM LEAVES

Notes

The Palm Tree holds great significance in the African culture. As sustenance, it provides food and drink. It provides shade from the sun; its roots are firmly implanted. The leaves can be used medicinally, eaten at times and used in making thatches that cover the roofs of homes.

But as endurable as it is, in parts of Ghanaian ethno-perspectives, the palm tree and its leaves symbolize "unity" and "creativity". Drawing from these, we titled this anthology.

Three poets, crafting their creative writing from a variety of sources; three poets, passing along some of the age old wisdom, symbolic of the ancient palm tree.

Part I

*15 poems by **Nana Arhin Tsiwah**

These Are Mothers: Some Dead, Some Alive

Mansa,
      when your tongue
punctuates the albums
of my tempering soul,
would I still not embrace
the pocket of announcements
of your lamenting lips
fondling my forehead
like a tender baby
in a bucket of
water?

Mensima,
      ornamental skies have slept
with a certain sadness
foamed in their eyes.
beautiful are the children
these soiled-covered legs
that carry pots of words
and serve sleeping tales
in broken calabashes

Baduwa,
       long dashes have risen
their log tongues of praise
they live in troubled huts;
with bleeding guts.
a child was heard crying
with cymbals of broken prayers
just as you waved past the muted tree
for the wounds of her birth
are still fresh
on the lensical openings

Mmba,

>
> we have not finished
> singing our songs

our harmonized verses
have pierced the ceilings
of our mouths
like dared kola nut,
you chew more and still no
home of solace is found
in the cabins of
the mouth

do not lament
>
> orphan breasts

that sings of bruised
wounds

do not break
those soft virgin canoes
that ploughs the hymen
of your eyes

o' child of a
>
> circumcised tongue

for the fall of every moon
comes with the scar
of a reborn one

Rented Cowries

when our memories die
under the navels
of our sons,
would we not
lace our hearts
    with tunes of
    a miraged
    tomb?

forged forgery fence,
have you no lips
to anchor your tongue
when the sea
corrodes with
salt?

    he lifts ebiasa under
    the chant of mbio
    he square two
    on the spring
        of *Wukuda*
        yet *Memenda*
    is still a bruised
    hymen...

    *Wukuda -- Mfantse-Akan for Wednesday
    *Memenda - Mfantse-Akan for Saturday

This Home: A Warmed Song

history would teach men
the beautiful arts
in collective war songs
that broke the
wheels of nations
and drained
the blood of orphans

poetry would teach men
that magical lanterns
can still light
the eyes
of dead bodies

There is a song we cannot sing at night.
it's sour and sordid under wet tongues
There is a music we cannot listen to calmly.
it echoes pains in violated blood lines
There is a road we cannot completely travel.
it slips beaded waists in chapters
There is a story we cannot finish writing.
it ruins libation in bottled-dirge...

like the tears of a dead
pregnant woman,
the pain is endless
even when its
nakedness stills
our feet on this
traced path—

When We Have Reached Home

maame would tell us *Anansesem*
and oil our ears with *Abakosem*
paapa would mentor our feet
with disinfested war dance
and give us edible elegies in
Atentenben.

for in this home,
    only drums of old
           gleam under
                  dark huts.

when we have crossed this lake
without purchased canoes
and death not befriended us,
we shall tell this tale once more
to the ears of our sons
to the hearts of our daughters
this tale shall find its feet
when we have
reached home safely...

        Home's Map
      even if i am lost
      deep inside these
      mischievous eyes
      of the forest
        that sang no song
          to the lonely bird,
            i shall find this road

i shall navigate
through plastic imprints
of cities that swallowed villages
of chapels that replaced oracles
of pharmaceuticals that waned herbs

even if i had lost
these footprints
that lean afar
smoking through
the corridors of nostrils
as days birth
memories of cold
nights

i shall winnow this chaff
under the feel of the sun-
this chaff that encodes
feigned foreign forage dreams
until that lost home
is found--

Three Hundred Fables

                We wrote her a song
                And he sung them
                Through his brass
                long nose

                She found her soul
                Calculated in long lines
                Of many pruned miles
                Knitted in summaries of
                Gloom.

                And when we had written her off
                Like a lullabied festivity,
                She wrote back
                In deep sentimental colours

*...She's found peace in this
sacramental ART of dying*

A Traveler's Recital

where we have reached
    we cannot tell
the stories told behind
our menopausal ears

we have found distilled
    meanings
to these stories
no one told us of

we have seen glowing
histories
that fight no more
hands on heart-breaks

and where we've reached,
our feet tap
    at wooden doors;
the stories we were told,
    before our departure,
became deepened lies.

Confrontational

He hummed a song of freedom
And found splattered
    hearts
of doom!
                He played an accordion
                And heard supplications
                of famed libation
                chants

Five days after the election,
His navel found
   A cued music
                Under a broken wooden bench
                The song was so
                alive that
                he returned no more to our
                mad house...

Salaga

I.
I cannot say we have finally arrived
Or look into the eyes of the Sun-God
And whisper memories of sunset
That we have, at last, been off-loaded

There is this sad-sweat streaming
It is the stream of six verses
Of six silent dirges
And caged in the memories of six parrots...

II.
How come the storm laid its axe of fury
Against the oldest baobab of our minds
When we laced the dilemmas of reflections
With each chain chained to her waist?

I can see all; the speaking tongues
Of broken walls, mud fenced faces
An old half-swallowed pond,
A dejected, solemnized graveyard;
The well and hand-drilled plates
Echoing the deeper silent tearful memories...

III.
A while beforehand,
You have cursed nature's pride,
Brutalised souls and poured
Pains of days and nights
Into the feet and hands
That never angered the bull's horn

Salaga,
Six verses plead
Six forged laments
Prayers and answers, laid in affliction
Hearts and walls, stood adjoined
With placebos of fate and faith
Drawing their tongues of echoed memoria...

Badu

*For the tenth Mfantse male born child

hatched sandstone,
hard-singled grain
that passed through
    patched soil,

Awotwe was not a curse
    he sprinkled water,
Nkrumah was an eye
    he watched even in sleep

till your bed was
spread with potassium,
Esoun mulched with sweat
    every leaf, weed; dung

Manu could have worn
the beads of jealousy,
Anan could have dug
    pot-holes along the stretch

I have seen those deep
indelible footprints
like a tractor's teeth
that Mensah left at shore,
symbols that Duku
shall soon foam
    where you fell...

Afarfo

      storms gossip
      with raging winds,
tides speak
in-lows; in-highs

      mountains build
      out of drunken waters,
      the sea cascades
      under canoes;

over-head
sweat mixes saliva,
open intestines leak
      as night falls; day draws
      till incessant muscles smiles...

            Afarfo – fishermen

Ekuafo

    the rains have
ceased to pour; to snore;
awaiting hearts in noon,
they lie indifferent
under grimaced clouds

    baked earth,
worms refuse to vomit
on gritty grains of soil,
leaves in-attentive
silence have quaked

    distill silent breaths
grace browned shrubs
scrap and screen,
till golden tubers
are milked.

Ekuafo -- farmers

Antobam

featherless duckling,
you chirp not
for the song of a beetle
erodes flowers of nectar

maame held her breath
like golden spider eggs,
she carved her lips into barks
taking in paapa's
midnight fragrance

it is not the forest
that is troubled,
when the hunter
lights a match
it's the trees

in the upper course,
erosion encodes
in the middle,
weight gathers
in the lower,
deposition is endured

be calm, be calm
for the winds
shall bleach time;
alter tides.

*Antobam - a child born with a deceased father

Abrebrese

I was not told...

I.
Paapa should have
told me of this impending
rain which shall wash
the leopard's spots away
Maame should have
cracked my ears with nuts
that i shall meet
this slicking sun on
harmattan's trails

II.
i. have. seen
laughing mattocks
eat me like mushrooms
from the mouth of a mound.
i. have witnessed
melting sun
rain on me and I was mute.

III.
an enemy i have
become in my own home
a bleeding rag i have
become in my own kitchen
with reddened hair strands,
palm oil is un-colourful

IV.

who is the deliverer
that shall swallow
this augury from
a solemn calabash?
i ask from this ghostly
fields of the hunter..

Abeberese -- a sufferer

Plea Without Help

With our cymbal lips,
    we have capsized this canoe.
the paddles are floating far away
and we are drowning deeper into its belly...

Tano looks helpless......
the venomous fishes
    are eating our toes!
we have become foes
and no soul
saves a foe!

I wish a swimmer
    comes-by with a CANOE
I pray a diviner passes-by
with anthills of COWRIES.
    Oh, who shall pour libation
to appease on
our behalf?

PART II

*15 Poems by **Nene Tetteh Adusu**

A Great Tree

During creation,
Seven great trees stood tall on earth
And with time they started bearing fruits
But now,
A great tree stands odd.
Many of its fruits are falling off
Because it has not been well fed

Many great farmers like Nkrumah tried
To bind them together but futilely.
The seeds of the fruits
Are not replanted to replicate a thousand fold
Making bacteria to fight among themselves.

Owners of the fruits when all but
The winds are dead:-
"The meek shall inherit the earth",
Is the scripture that rang in their heads.
After centuries of freedom, has the
Reign of the meek begun?

Frogged.

I am the frog who cannot hop
Over the tinniest clap of sand
So I walk like a bat-
Blindly.

Did mother sleep with a bat?
The possibility I long to understand
But my full I featured body of frog
Walks but never hoping.

I wonder—
How many siblings do I have?
Did mother give out the springs
Before I came?

I am the frog who wants to hop
Over flint stones in the savannah
Croak loudly to tell the winds—
I am the frog who can hop.

Candle

A candle
Stands on a hill
Melting time away
In gentle flickering fire.

It burns down
Bruising itself: polished
And shiny.

A candle
Burns, burns, burns
And hurts in the end,
Itself and its holder.

Today: Tomorrow

Today,
We stand at the castle road,
Casting our eyes back
The independence is evident
Cast our minds back
Vassalage rules!

Today,
We march on Obestsebi's skin,
We march
We put on Obestsebi's skin,
Ahead, we march
To the reassurance of nothingness.

Today,
We look back
Wail in the freedom of venality
As we curse today.

Today,
Faith rules, unvoted for,
As democracy and freedom sit in selfishness.

Today,
Births tomorrow!
Tomorrow begins
Today!

Nightmare

Nightmares
What pictures they are?

Nightmare,
A journey taken with no fare.

Nightmare,
A fear evocation which craves a spiritual air.

Nightmare,
Horrenfic action like riding a mare

Nightmare,
Reality shake hands with dreams,
An act so fare

Nightmare
A fearful premonition...

Africa: *Slowly* And *Quietly*

Slowly and quietly,
The wheel of patriotism
Is rolling out of Africanism.

Slowly and quietly,
The wheels of corruption,
The wheels of selfishness,
All, loftily and grandly roll in.

Slowly and quietly,
The people are indifferent,
The leaders are different,
Untied are our aspirations-
Preach Yes and live No.

Slowly and quietly,
The angry winds of modernity
are quietly eroding our hard won freedom
Back into a disguised form of colonisation.

Slowly and quietly,
Patriotism thrives in our history
And more citizens want to be characters
Yet our sweats are now tears,
Unwiped still.

PALM LEAVES

Quickly and loudly,
Slowly and quietly
The winds of change blow
From a distant land,
Unsought for in this land.

Quickly and slowly
Loudly and quietly
Let change tumble and rumble from our *Obonu*,
And our leaders dance our identity
Like *AkɔM*, possessed
and *Kete*, royally beautiful
And the people follow suite.
Quickly and loudly!

*Obonu- a Ga drum
AkɔM- a ritual dance
Kete- an Asante royal dance.

One More Hymn (For Kofi Awoonor)

The Earth's Brother, mouthpiece of
tradition, a potent wayfarer,
virgin's envy
ferried across the river of tears,
you are away in the land across ours.
In the explosion and exhibition of
thunderous fireworks at The Gate,

our world became dark,
the explosion was colourful
full of absurdism and beingness-
butchered meat was sent in splinters
down to the earth.
What is the beingness of a dead meat?
The sound of the flute is chaotic.
Ears seem not to hear nor eyes to see
the flute's dripping tears.
They killed you but never killed you,
for tomorrow, a decade and scores of years
to come, my children

And their children's children will know
that huge senseless cathedral of doom,
Rediscovering their true selves
and communing with *Sika*
In the new found land.
In your words of mine-

It cannot be the explosion we heard that night
that still lingers in the chambers of memory,
It is the new chorus of poetry
And the acts of our second selves.
The fallen tree carried off by the rain
dries in the sun,
wrapped in the earth, your brother.
I sit brooding over the scars left
by your exodus.

Peace, Where It Lies?

      Where does peace lie?
Is it that light aired garden
where trees wave troubles Goodbye
And sing lullabies to sorrows?

Is it standing by the soft, clean
Flowing stream, so fresh,
Quietly lugging angst along?

Is it kneeling in prayer,
Rendering clothes
and throwing weighted conscience
In the face of deities?

Is it the self-fulfilling of conscience
Which cannot be reaved by laws,
so selfish and unjust?

Is it the silence after a shot?
That silence,
Or the silence, blessed
by the transcendence of a soul?
Any soul; all souls!
      Where lies the peace?

A Sin, Poverty

wake up every morning
to the sun of hope
blinding in anguish.
the fortitude of life,
a hexed ram for the altar,
alters not a sin as poverty.

poverty; is it a sin?
a curse deeded to the poor?-
inflicted pain casting
the poor to the lake of suffering
with skimpy, bruised
contusions of selves-
the spirit craves
for food like the flesh.
is this the inheritance promised?

bread is anguish
and
water is poison.

wealth grows in the garden of the rich,
yet not in the farms of the poor.

Ire

Ire
burns like inclement fire.

Anger like red,
Volcanizing blood,
Teetering feet,
Racing thoughts unfinished,
Face creaks and cracks,
Fingers marry unity,
Inaudible; mumbled speeches.

Culminating...
Rising...
Released!

Normalcy visits,
Stability stays,
Thoughts meet senses,
Regrets rent the heart
The lips say kiss sorry,
Forgiveness is birthed,
Amidst mirth.
It's done!

Anger, like red,
Burns taciturnly!
Burns quietly
Burns ....
Dangerously

Disquiet

That sky cried blew into my being
I wallowed blindly in myself
To search the water in me
To hold me down to this earth.

The sun dried the river in me
Empty am I in myself.

Windy! Bobbling!
The blood in my veins.
I exist

But in torments scaled on me
I hold my pain to the thin air-
Only to be....

Watered by the sky,
Dried by the sun
Blown by the wind

I pray thee
Wind to wind-
Blow away!

Stolen Moments

Moments slipped past the wall
built with straw corner stones.

A wavering wall like a leaf
dropped from a tree lowly stood:
blown by the wind.

Moments stolen
by one ignorant of thievery,
but a thief knows not a gift
nor appreciates freedom.

Broken

Sands of absence winds up into my eyes
My pupil run into the classroom of my eyes,
As my hands nonchalantly stagger by my body,
To scratch my eyes and free my pupil,
But i couldn't,
Now, I'm blinded for no fault of mine.
The rains tear down from the sky,
I felt it pat the roofy eyelids
With its genial water,
Sluggishly opening up the world to me again,
Rains of presence have flooded my eyes,
Now i see, by no fault of mine.

Joy Lost Found

'Twas dark and empty,
Shining and bright she was,
Making darkness yield
To light's field.

In her eyes
Was my long lost joy,
Last seen days ago
in those same eyes.

Her smile,
Irritatingly Beautiful
With teeth, well aligned,
Like trumpeting angels.

In her embrace,
My heart runs a race,
An endless race
To destinations unknown.

In her presence
I'm so me
Letting myself go
Like the blue above.

The dust refuses
To be mud!
Rain drops,
Thud! Thud! Thud!

Caressing dust,
Gently,
Making love to it.
Now,
Mud!

Gazing, Glancing, and Guessing.

From the roots,
Stretch up by creaks,
With little cracks
Of light.

Then,
A fore sight of branches,
Inviting me for crunches,
Held by the hand
I see the eyes,
Which make my eyes
The old wears-out,
then the fresh
Becomes apparent,
Displaying your green,
I expressed restrain
To await you,

The day I look you in the eye,
Am out of your reach.
Awaken to life
By the sound of your strife,
Then, there you were
I see your bruises for the sweetest.

Part III

*15 poems by **Kofi Acquah**

In The Silent River

The silent river
is not dry to sack the fisherman
And when the baskets of borbor traders
Become too heavy to cross
By the canoe
Even though they need not,
They invite a second hand.

The hunting mouth is in trouble
to meddle with affairs
Of inmates' silent goddesses of the river
If she pours a hot oil
On their cold toes,

For they calm the tickled ribs
Of the wicked roaming ancestor
When they roar

Infants bubble with joyful mouths
Just when the dancing priest
In the family's shrine is tamed.

Who then shall call the rain to make a hay?
And feet on the sands of the desert;
For thousands of miles and live?
O'! Except the camel may

PALM LEAVES

It twinkles in here
like the lights of Christmas 'nock-outs
And the days jingle
in Amandzeba's single

On the silent river
comes a romantic discourse
A romantic discourse
and romantic dialogues
Falling from within the jaws
Of the river's ripples

Come you, O' passer-by come!
And do swear not an oath
For her tide falls gently
As honey
slowly flows in her cleavage

Pass on safe, again and again
That,
You shall call many
to take on the sail
For the sword is thrusted
Deep inside the river

O' Passer-by
I say, come!
Pass on safe, again and again
On the silent river.

Yaanom

How hard shall the snail chuckle
To soften the pains of our sword filled mouths?

Yaanom,
Should plagues plague the palace plate?
And deny the glass to slake the king's throat?

Yaanom,
Would fireflies under hurricane lamps
Die in their torn sacks and shoes?
Whilst the light shines for good

O' Yaanom,
When do these licking tongues
Halt a pounce to great hidden thoughts of sages?

Yaanom,
Listen to scoop from pukes
Then bisect the lines to see the length

Yaanom shall make your foot a messenger
To sit on post
Then forsake the sweat and mind not
when you tell the aggrieved tale.

A Broken Pot

A spittle from a red tongue
falls on a rock and dies
A throat is fading away
by a constant shout;
pulling the intestines out
As he opens his jaws wide
like a cock crows at five

These mere cracks,
on the rough dying mud walls
In the forest's core,
seem to catch each high call

As at dawn,
the soft wrinkled palms of grandpa
Would pat his back and frown
and all pester him for one reason
But,
what season feels his feelings?

For the tick-tock of the clock
only evokes a sound of teasing
As the masters of the top
enter and exit
With sacks filled with ear tingling lyrics
of comfort breeze as promised

Yet,
his voice and dreams
Keep swinging on pawpaw trees
Whilst,
on mirror grounds they cruise

Shadows From The West

Veins appearing and disappearing
Muscles harden; by days
Kano clothes; then are made
from these falling, black, thickened sweats
Dropping and pulsating in the western plate

When sands of the Saharan desert cry,
And oases; survive the camels' throat
Then gold for swords,
Ivory for figs,
shells, cowries, and salts for wealth
this, tightened the western pockets

If the ancient clock tickles thus,
then
Memories and feelings fickle by
From the influencers' kitchen
to the village huts
where bellies fell

For the symbols and shadows
of the native traders
Still lurk in his eyes
leaving indelible marks
of something belonging
to guilt
deep in his conscience

Stuck to the fetish

He watches
when grandpa incantates
Swallowing seeds like pills
Consciously, these memories
Etch; forming his essence

Then at a tender age
he says;
Fortify me
To escape.
Bath me, O' bath me!
So I can be

Tied to his waist; an amulet
A Talisman
resting below his abdomen
Soft ribs throb
now gather courage

Moments after his shadow
Enemies wallow
He claims ownership
of things he never owes
For who dares test his throat?
While he,
now abides in
The Gods' home?

Fie Nyimpa

When you rattle your beads
You feast among the beasts
Lovers,
think quick escaping feet for your breath unknown

Yet,
there you secretly lean
With lustful teeth
to prey on same meat

When the cracking earth
Hear the ears,
this diverted fate,
Becomes a rag to the victim

As Aba and Ammba
cry sympathy,
Of whom they cry about
Buries them in reply

Fie nyimpa!
You advise the eyes up to the sky
And torment them
to despise the ground
For you're a trap setter
Catching and sucking from our ankles

You perforate our bodies
With fangs sharp as knives
you're sneaky, a creeper
who knows
That,
The hen sees not its anus.

Fie nyimpa
We clear the weeds today
To see what lies within your hay

Under The Village Hut

It takes heart under this hut
For strangers to dance to our covered sounds
Only the 'dondo' keeps company
Thus, wipes away the piercing memories of harm

In thorns and dingy sacks
I search the last mango to suck
But tired like a chased cock;
I blurred in a falling fog

When mushrooms scatter
Tearing apart in haste their shades
At the sight
Of our torn stinking flour sack cover
My chest pounds
Then,
The earth begin to sink me
In shame and sweats

Ah! Mena Aba!
Here I now bend
In Nana's bequeathed egyakoto
For the shackles of today
Seem to stand to threaten

But tomorrow
The parrot shall tell them
That,
Under the village hut
Still will many eyes see
From this lamentation

Koryɛ

Asaase yi mmpow ne dze
Ntsi hwɛ ɛ,
Kutu yi yɛ hɛn baasa dze

We tie not our waist
To fight a bond
For envy at the time
Counted wrong

From the unborn
To Abeiku to Kofi to ɛkɔw
Unearthed the single pond
Different fishes, yet in the same pond

Why should Adwoa inscribe on each?
For her womb even bears a witness
To spitting no spittle on none at birth
For she said;
Go tri-head and come tri-leg

Kutu yi
yɛ hɛn baasa nyina dze
I charge you,
You beyond my belly
To split not, fight not
But keep the blood and oneness bond
For hate to hurt
Heals back not, the wound

I will sigh in rest
For the dust assures a soft whirl
Till ɔbɔ adze calls
Unity to peace, do strenghten

Pull The Trigger

I trot hastily with dying feet
into the casket
of ɔkofo Yaa Asantsewaa
To scoop that indelible inspiration
left in the sack of the courageous

I see the pawpaw tree
Sway before the farmer with
undying confidence
For when legends are invoked
Lost hopes come home

The Village Boys

We listen less to our masters
For our hearts yearn
for the cry of the closing drum
And quicken to where our joy come

Grandpa's promise
Lingers on our minds
So we run like horses
To the thatched hut
for busy hands and busy mouths

O' Village life teaches us
More than the classroom
For we tend to know best
Of our world

PALM LEAVES

The deer hunting
The morn crab catching
The night snail searching
The twilight story telling
The circle circle
The birds catapulting
Yɛnkɔhwɛ Adwoa Ata
Na neho tse sɛn ni
And the bonfire don't stop burning

We are not savages and pagans
We are proud of our cutlasses and guns
Though,
The right eye
Seem to seek the squirrel
for high marks
Yet,
We are still the village boys

Here We Sit

We are tomorrow's eye
Mama,
You would say with your voice high
But,
Could birds of the sky fly
Without wings at their backs?

Yesterday,
You drained our tears with painted hopes
But we see through your eyes
That,
you were just sealing your back
As good times you daily wish us

What do we do
To the hidden coffers in the sand of our land?
Mama!
Here we sit, we're not sick
But these empty calabashes
we hold now
From morn till night
We drink back our tears
and eat our fears
We remember the swords and spears;
And all the bloodshed.

So would Paapa be glad,
To see Kofi fold his arms behind the traffic?
Whilst he,
Softly bounces in the four wheel drive?

O' Maame!
We sit under your warm arms
Listen to our cry
And tell Paapa,
Tell Paapa!
Tell Paapa!
We say, tell Paapa.
For our eyes are swimming
in this rippling river on our cheeks

Jumping The Pit

Long have I remained
behind the pit
And of a loose tongue
I force to sip

Little by little; dots of thoughts
I'm jumping the pit
Freeing the kids
And by the dew falling ends
Shall I polish the black shoe
With bestowed woven words.

Cultured Old Days

Times began with manners
For little ones
Emptied the head of the old
They left in their hands only the machete
To leave the strength to hold

For they knew best- the elderly
And served each above equally
They sought grey hairs easily
And the old gave, whole heartedly

Nothing was hate
Different sons
Were each his
The sun,
At last blessed with a kiss
O' ! Nice were those days

When hungry,
one saw a fruit and plucked it
To everybody, everything belonged
Beside each pathway banana laid
To anywhere can carry anyone along
I love to see again those days

Preservers

Rain like cane whips
Falling as I carry down my woven basket
but hiding places abound
For trees grew broader leaves

Within shorter days
Villagers sing bumper harvest
Corn barns are twisted
And hunters bring home smiles
from the forest

I saw them ancient
Preserving all the Maker made
In the natural way
but I see less
in this day

Laughing Cowries

He spreads on the floor
to deceive the poor
See the cowries laugh
O' see them laugh
Cowries are voice dumbs
But see the owner laugh

ABOUT CONTRIBUTING POETS

NANA ARHIN TSIWAH

Nana Arhin Tsiwah, is an undergraduate student of the University of Cape Coast-Ghana where he is reading Geography and Economics. As a disciple of Africanism Consciousness, Akan cultural ideology and elements in Akanism; Tsiwah, a linguist- performist of Mfante-Akan Traditional Ancestry writes from Cape Coast-Ghana. His works usually dwells on African-Cultural mysticism and unfolded folklores. Tuck magazine, Kreative Diadem, EXPOUND, Afri-Poet, Sypghana, Anansekrom, African Writer, Lunaris Review et al are some online hubs that have published his works. He is the Chief-Linguist in the Africanism poetry movement, "The Village Thinkers".
He blogs at www.nanaarhintsiwah.wordpress.com

NENE TETTEH ADUSU

Writing under his indigenous name- **Nene Tetteh Adusu**, Tetteh- a Poet, Performer and dramatist, hails from Ghana and currently lives in Accra. He opines that - just as words were used in creating this world, so can the world be transformed by words. Mirroring life and crashing them when necessary to fit the pieces in life's dazzling puzzle- his philosophy. Nene holds an B.A (Hons.) Theatre Arts from the University of Cape Coast, Ghana. He was the "Order of the Village" awardee at The Village Thinkers Poetry Honorary Awards, 2015.

KOFI ACQUAH

Eduful Ishmael, known in literary creative circles as *'Kofi Acquah'* is one refined voice of poetic and artistic word-score. Born in May 1994, Kofi Acquah hails from Ajumako-Bisease but had his basic education at Heritage Academy-Breman Essiam and is currently a final year student of Bisease Senior High School in the Central Region of Ghana. Having devised the art of creative and imaginative writing at a tender age, Kofi has not only progressed in play writing, literary sketching, and story-writing but has on a tenacious forthrightness through a serene literary scale equally placed his art under the lethal eyes of poetry. Thus, a linguist-brewed voice as a poet-wordist (poetry performer). His profound ink of deeper mysticisms, sentimentalism and critical life; echoing tunes under the balm of poetry, leave nuggets of imprints in the mind of the reader. This has thus, earned him a certificate in an online American Poetry Marathon show. Some of his works have appeared on prominent literary online publications. Such as; Poetry Soup, African Literature on facebook (where he won its maiden poetry competition for African poets), Poem Hunter, Stage Afrik, an interview on The Village Thinker, Lunaris Review and Best New Poems.

COMING SOON!!!!

Blood Tied - Nene Tetteh Adusu

Sound of the Tsetse Drum - Kofi Acquah

www.ingramcontent.com/pod-product-compliance
Lightning Source LLC
Chambersburg PA
CBHW060658030426
42337CB00017B/2671